Logical Reasoning

2

www.pegasusforkids.com

Published by Kuldeep Jain for B. Jain Publishers (P) Ltd., D-157, Sector 63, Noida - 201307, U.P.
Registered office: 1921/10, Chuna Mandi, Paharganj, New Delhi-110055

Printed in India

Contents

Chapter 1: Pattern Completion........5

Chapter 2: Measuring Unit........11

Chapter 3: Geometrical Shapes........16

Chapter 4: Grouping........23

Chapter 5: Special Understanding........29

Chapter 6: Ranking Test........35

Answer Key........40

PREFACE

Logical Reasoning is an interesting and innovative series of six books, which will enhance the thinking skill of a child. This series will sharpen a child's mind and by practising the questions on regular basis, the child's brain will undergo a mental workout.

The presentation and the progressive learning process of the series makes solving the questions an enjoyable experience. A student develops a habit of thinking logically with daily practice. The series also strengthens the mental mathematics skills and help children to solve textbook level maths effortlessly. The questions are well-supported by icons, cartoon characters, and illustrations, making the series fascinating.

Each book has six chapters that focus on different aspects of thinking and make learning an easy and engrossing process. The various fascinating chapters include:

- Pattern completion
- Measuring units
- Geometrical shapes
- Grouping
- Ranking test
- Puzzle test
- Direction sense
- Time and calendar
- Coding-decoding
- Water and mirror images, etc.

We wind up this series with the hope that students, teachers and parents will appreciate our efforts and the students will practise the questions regularly. We invite constructive feedback for improvement of our future editions.

Pattern Completion

In the problems relating to Pattern Completion, one has to complete the patterns of letters, numbers, symbols, simple drawings or other figures. Let us practise completing some patterns here.

Choose the correct option in each of the following questions:

1. Which is the missing number in the following number pattern?

a. 15 b. 18 c. 20 d. 22

2. Which is the missing number pair in the following pattern?

a. 60, 61 b. 59, 61 c. 61, 63 d. 63, 65

3. **Which part will complete the given figure?**

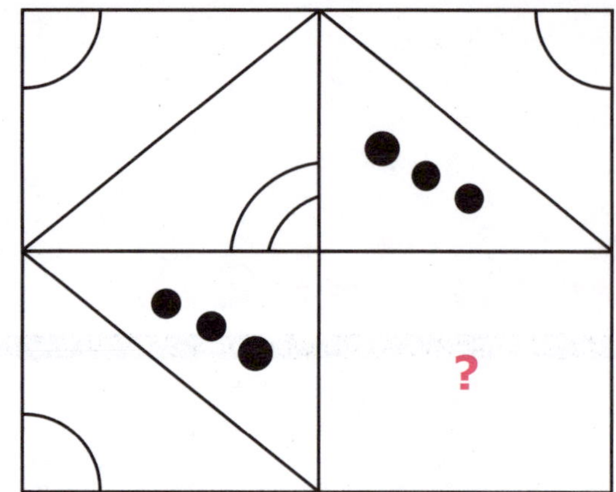

a. b. c. d.

4. **Find the next number in the following number pattern:**

a. 30 b. 20 c. 21 d. 25

5. **Find the missing number in the following number pattern:**

a. 10 b. 11 c. 12 d. 9

6. **Find the missing shapes in the following pattern:**

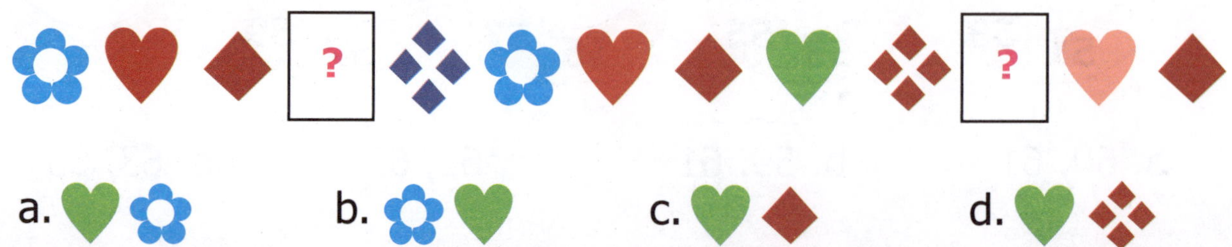

7. **Find the missing shape in the following pattern:**

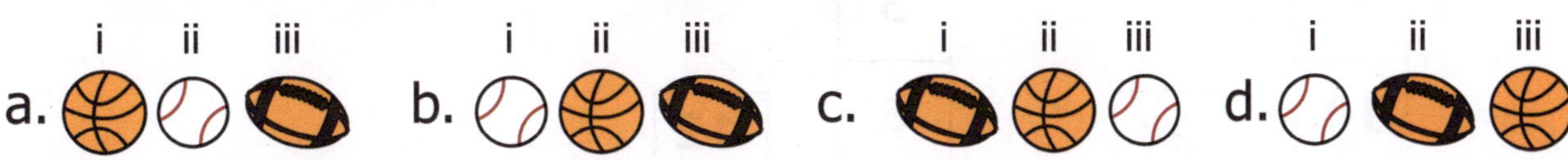

8. **Find the missing shape in the following pattern:**

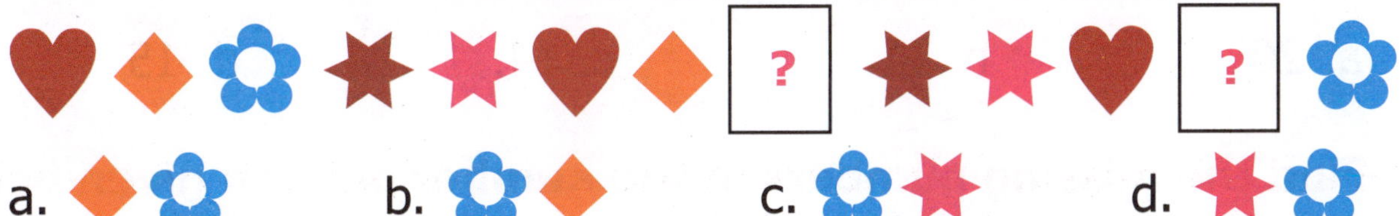

9. **Complete the figure pattern given below:**

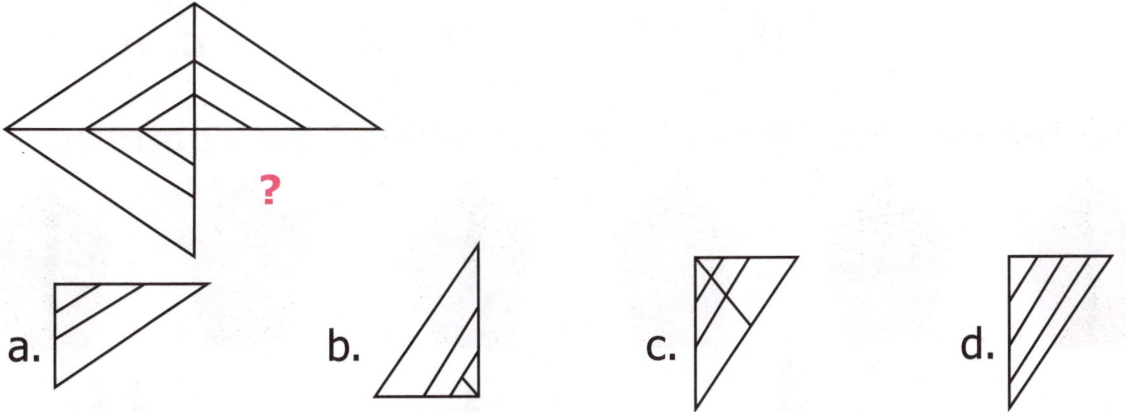

10. **Complete the figure pattern given below:**

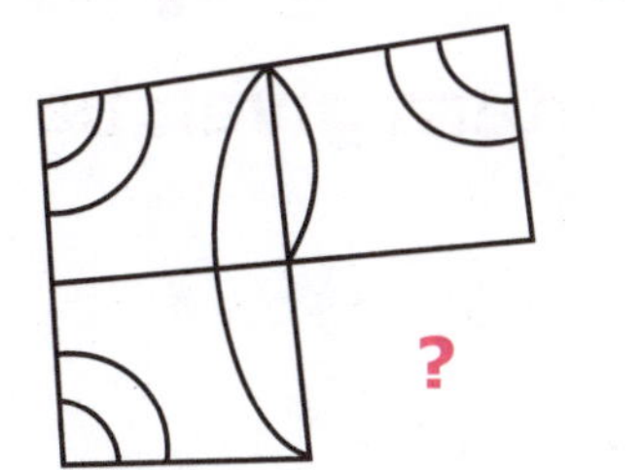

a. 

b. 

c. 

d. 

11. **Missing figures in the pattern given below are:**

a. b. c. d.

12. **Follow the pattern given in figure-I to find the missing number in figure-II:**

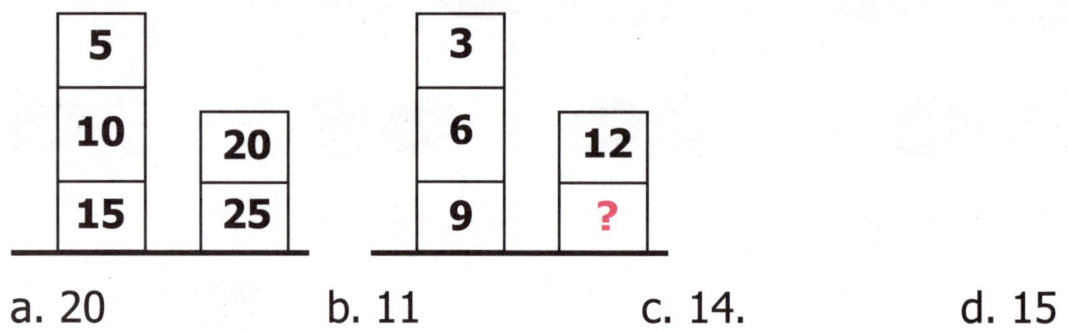

a. 20 b. 11 c. 14. d. 15

13. **Find the missing numbers in the number pattern given below:**

a. 20, 22 b. 18, 20 c. 16, 24 d. 20, 24

14. **Find the missing figures in the following figure pattern:**

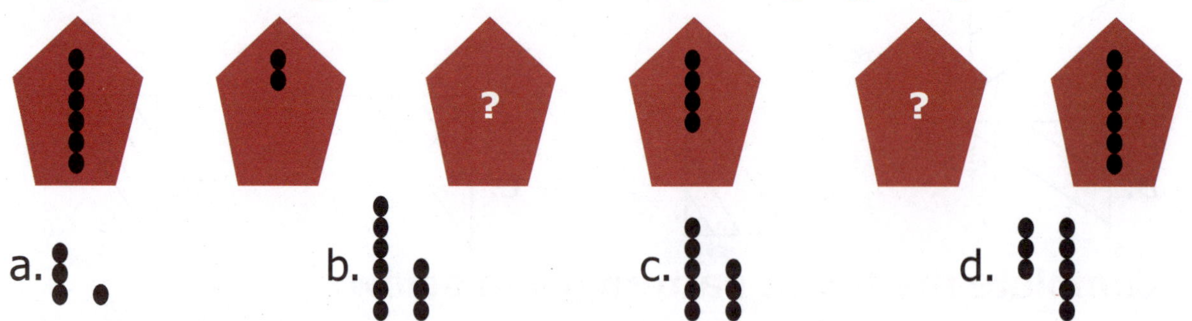

a. b. c. d.

15. **Find the missing number in the number pattern given below:**

5	10	5
2	4	2
3	?	3

a. 6 b. 9 c. 8 d. 10

16. **Find the missing figure in the pattern given below:**

a. b. c. d.

17. **Find the missing number in the number pattern given below:**

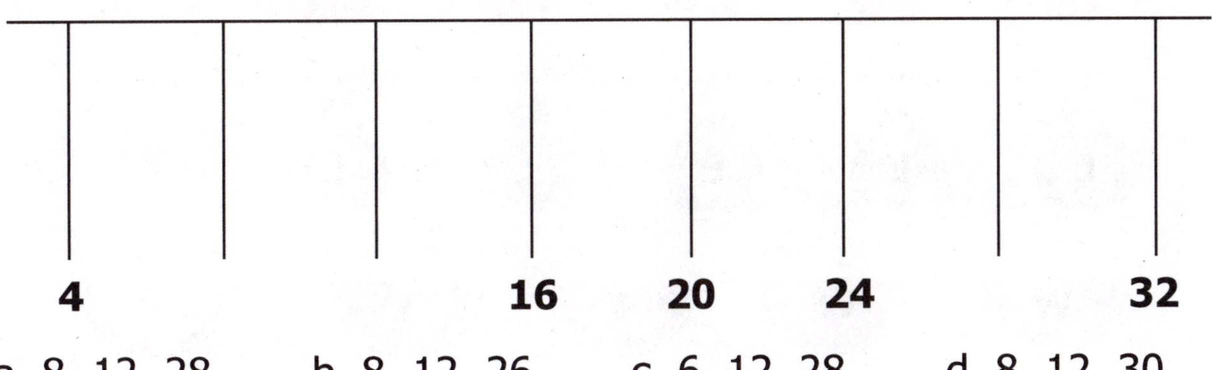

a. 8, 12, 28 b. 8, 12, 26 c. 6, 12, 28 d. 8, 12, 30

18. **Find the missing figure in the pattern given below:**

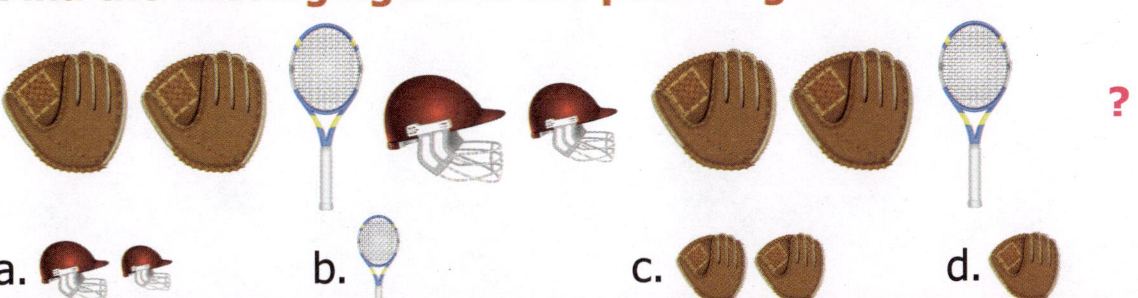

19. Find the missing figure in the patterns given below:

20. Find the missing letters in the letter patterns given below:

a. R, A, L, T b. R, P, L, W c. O, A, L, T d. R, P, E, W

Measuring Units

To measure anything, we have some specific units. These units are called measuring units.

For example: Milk is measured in litres, vegetables are measured in kilograms and length of an object is measured in centimetres. Long distances are measured in metres and kilometres, etc.

Choose the correct option in each of the following questions:

1. What is the length of the pencil?

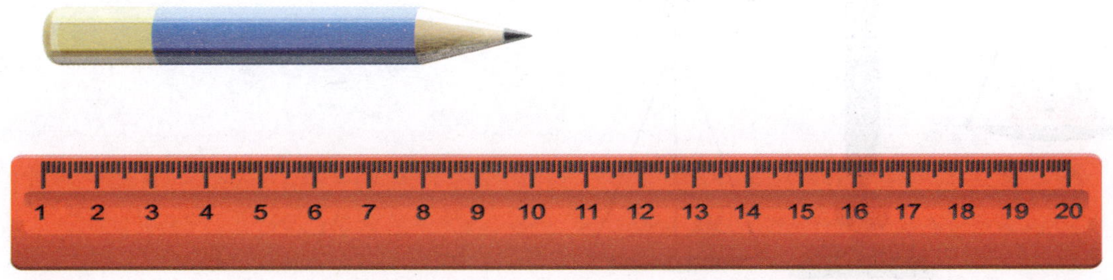

a. 10 cm b. 12 cm c. 14 cm d. 15 cm

2. Which of the following is the heaviest?

a.  b.  c.  d. 

3. If today is Sunday, the day after tomorrow will be ____________________.

a. Monday b. Wednesday c. Tuesday d. Thursday

4. At what time do we see the moon and the stars in the sky?

a. morning b. afternoon c. evening d. night

5. Which of the following is the tallest?

a.  b.  c.  d. 

6. The apples are __________ pineapple in the following figure.

a. heavier than b. lighter than c. as heavy as d. equals to

7. Which of the following objects is the lightest?

a.  b.  c.  d. 

8. Bananas are _____________ grapes in the following picture.

a. equals to b. lighter than c. as heavy as d. heavier than

9. Sheri's family is eating breakfast in the _______________.

a. morning b. afternoon c. evening d. night

10. A boy has $10. He saw a ball that costs $15. How much more money does he need to buy the ball?

a. $2 b. $5 c. $6 d. $10

11. Look at the picture carefully. The weighing machine is showing that:

a. Side A has more weight than side B
b. Side A has less weight than side B
c. Side A and side B have equal weight
d. Side B has less weight than side A

12. **How much time does the long hand of a clock take to complete its four rounds?**

a. 1 hour   b. 2 hours   c. 3 hours   d. 4 hours

13. **Look at the given fruit box. It has 16 fruits. Each fruit costs $2. How much will the entire box cost?**

a. $32   b. $40   c. $35   d. $42

14. **A jar can hold 2 cups of water. How many cups of water is necessary to fill 3 jars.**

a. 8   b. 6   c. 7   d. 10

Direction: Look at the picture given below and solve the questions from 15-17:

15. **The eraser is ____________ shorter than the pencil.**

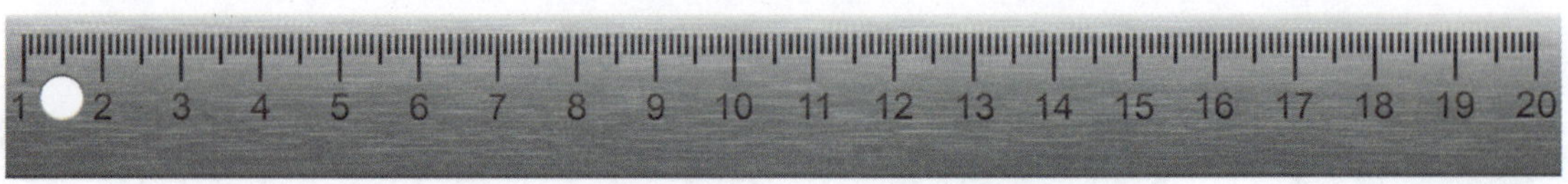

a. 11 cm   b. 10 cm   c. 12 cm   d. 14 cm

16. The length of the pencil is:

a. 15 cm   b. 12 cm   c. 13 cm   d. 14 cm

17. The pencil is ________________ shorter than the ruler.

a. 4 cm   b. 6 cm   c. 5 cm   d. 7 cm

Direction: Look at the picture given below and answer the questions that follow:

18. If (watermelon) = 1 kg then what is the weight of  ?

a. 6 kg   b. 4 kg   c. 5 kg   d. 3 kg

19. If (bucket) = (3 watermelons) then how many watermelons are required for (4 buckets) ?

a. 10   b. 12   c. 14   d. 16

20. If 1 glass = 90 ml, then the jug can hold ______ ml of water.

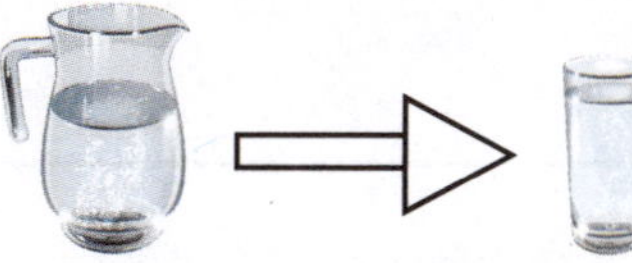      

a. 500 ml   b. 540 ml   c. 560 ml   d. 600 ml

Geometrical Shapes

Shapes

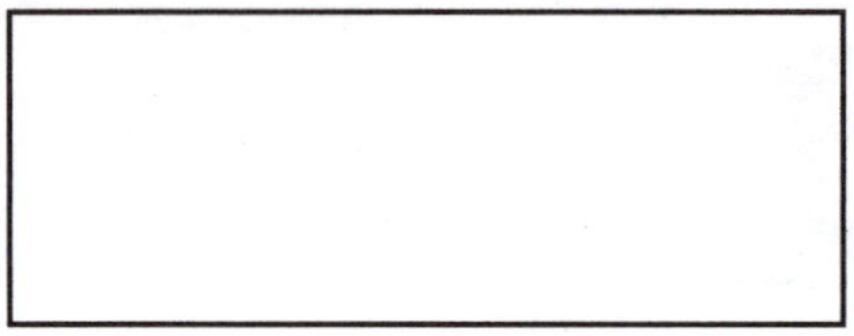

Rectangle

Circle

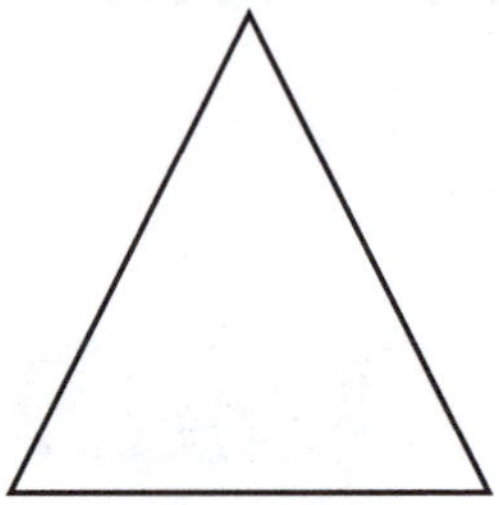

Triangle

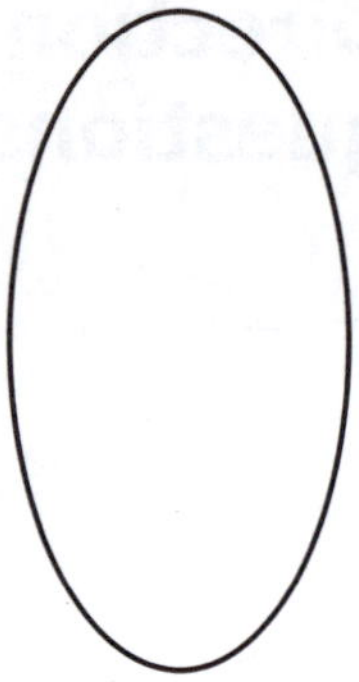

Oval

Square

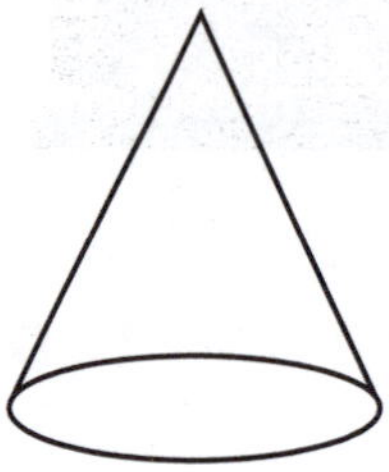

Cone

Cylinder

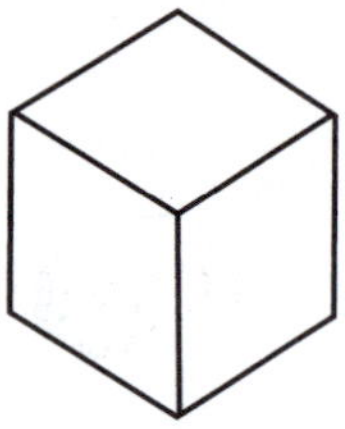

Cube

Lines

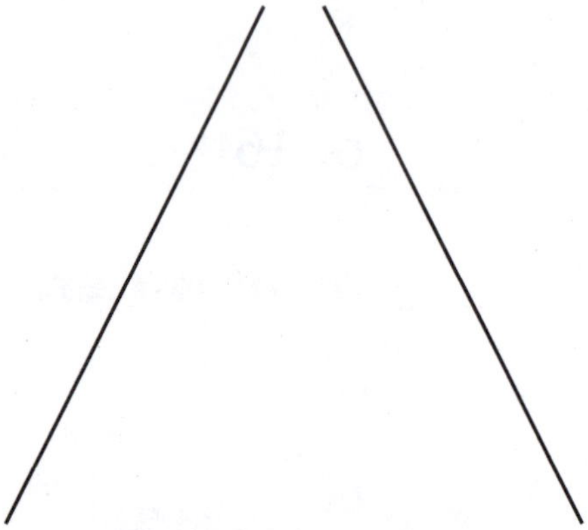

Curved line

Slanting lines

Vertical line

Horizontal line

Choose the correct option in each of the following questions:

1. Select the correct match:

A.		i.	Cube
B.	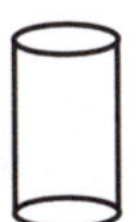	ii.	Triangle
C.	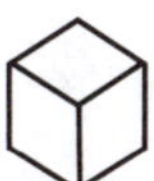	iii.	Cone
D.		iv.	Cylinder
E.		v.	Oval

a. A-iii, B-iv, C-i, D-v, E-ii
b. A-i, B-iv, C-iii, D-v, E-ii
c. A-iii, B-i, C-iv, D-v, E-ii
d. A-iii, B-iv, C-i, D-ii, E-v

2. Select the correct match:

A.		i.	Curved line
B.		ii.	Horizontal lines
C.		iii.	Vertical lines
D.		iv.	Slanting lines

a. A-iii, B-iv, C-i, D-ii
b. A-iv, B-iii, C-i, D-ii
c. A-iii, B-i, C-iv, D-ii
d. A-iii, B-iv, C-i, D-ii

3. There are ______________ more rectangles than triangles in the figure below.

a. 1 b. 2 c. 3 d. 4

Direction: Look at the picture given below carefully and answer the questions that follow:

4. There are ______________ triangles.

a. 9 b. 8 c. 5 d. 6

5. There are ______________ rectangles.

a. 9 b. 8 c. 5 d. 6

6. There are ______________ circles and triangles altogether.

a. 14 b. 15 c. 12 d. 13

Direction: Look at the picture given below and answer the questions 7-10:

7. There are ______________ circles and rectangles altogether.

a. 17 b. 18 c. 16 d. 15

8. There are ______________ triangles and squares altogether.

a. 6 b. 7 c. 8 d. 11

9. How many squares are there in the given figure?

a. 3 b. 4 c. 5 d. 6

10. How many circles are there in the given figure?

a. 3 b. 4 c. 7 d. 5

11. Select the correct option for:

i. Full figure ii. Shaded area

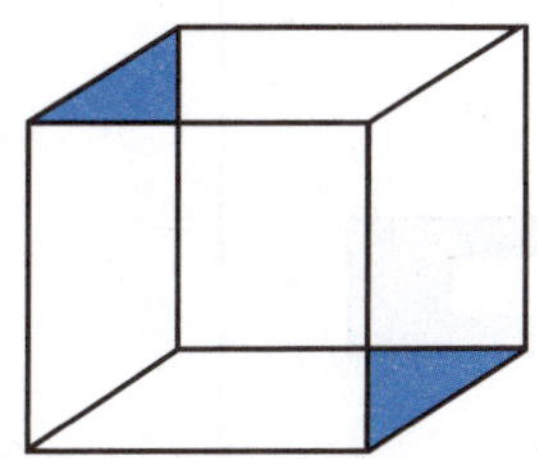

a. cube, rectangle
b. rectangle, triangle
c. cube, triangle
d. cylinder, triangle

12. Select the correct option for:

i. Full figure

ii. Shaded area

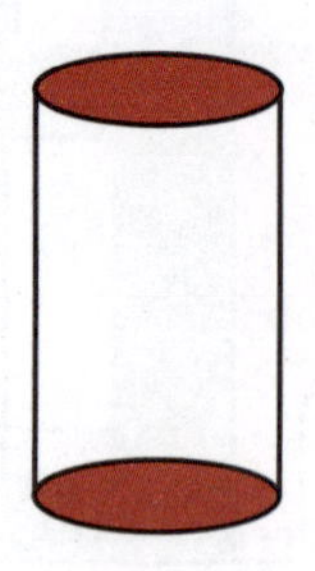

a. cube, rectangle

b. cylinder, triangle

c. cube, oval

d. cylinder, oval

13. Select the correct option for:

i. Full figure

ii. Shaded area

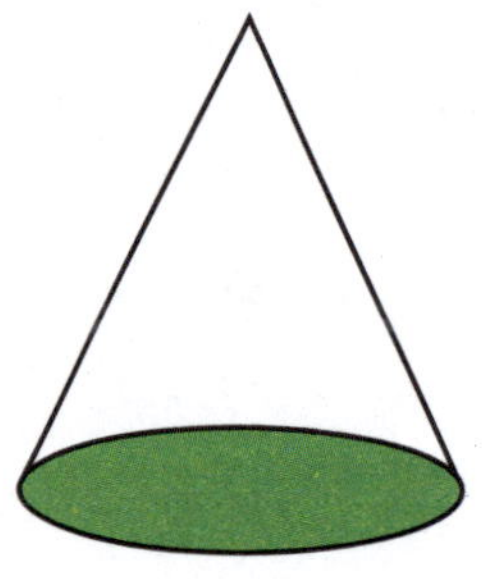

a. cone, oval

b. cylinder, triangle

c. cube, oval

d. cylinder oval

14. The following figure has ______________ squares.

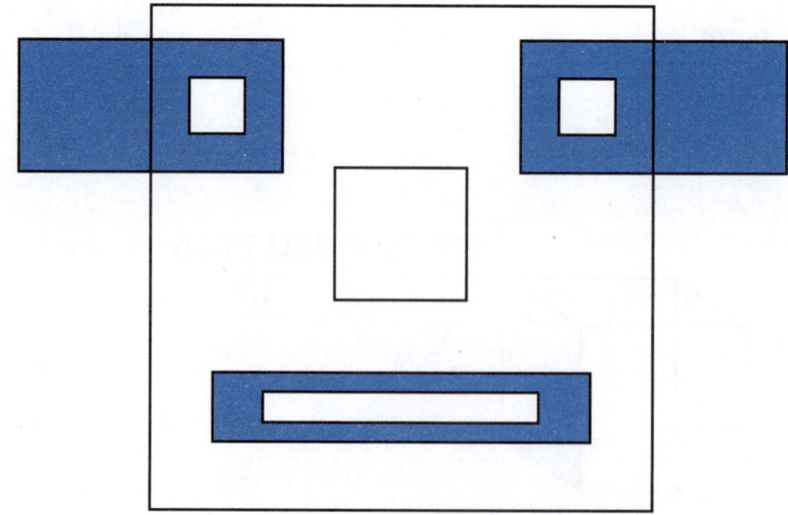

a. 10 b. 8 c. 11 d. 12

15. **Which two figures should combine to form a square?**

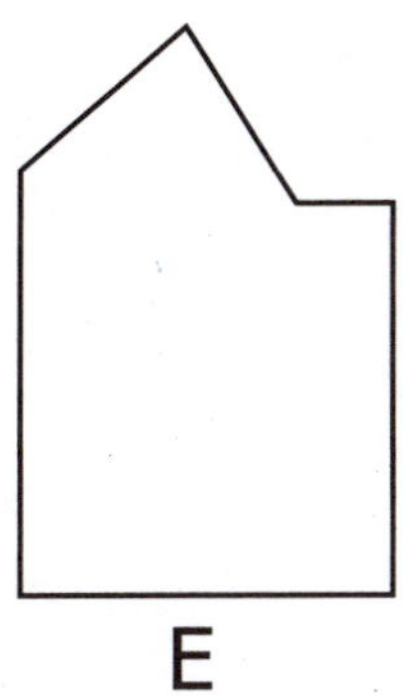

E

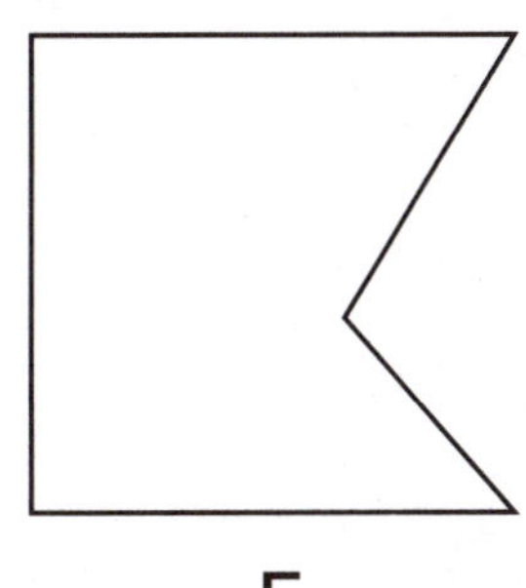

F

C

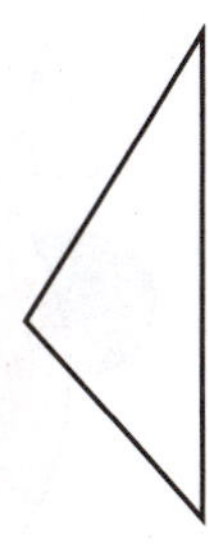

H

a. E and H b. F and E c. F and H d. E and G

Direction: Look at the following shapes for question 16-17:

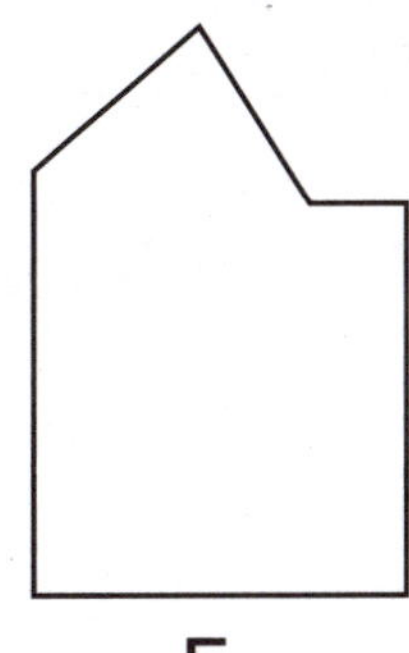

E

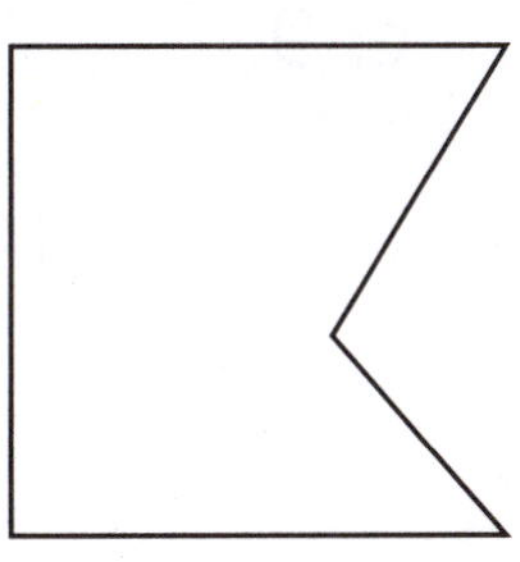

F

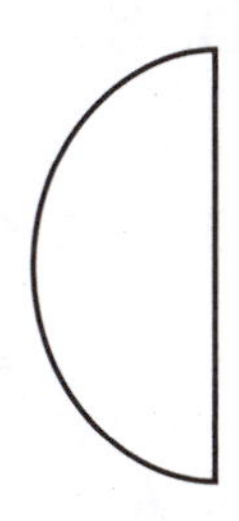

G

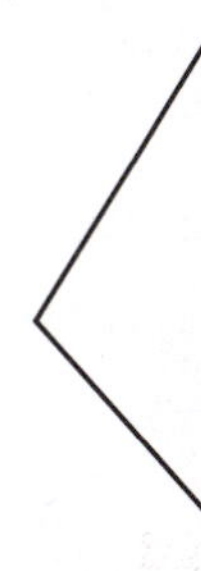

H

16. **How many slanting lines has the figure F?**

a. 2 b. 3 c. 4 d. 5

17. **How many slanting lines have been used to make the figure E?**

a. 1 b. 2 c. 3 d. 4

18. **How many standing lines and curved lines are used to make following two figures?**

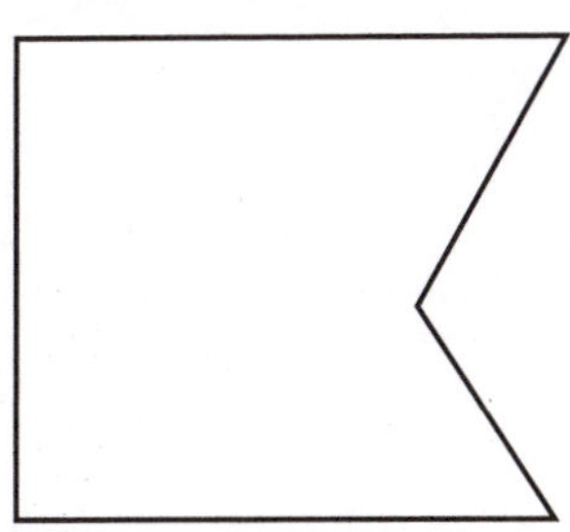

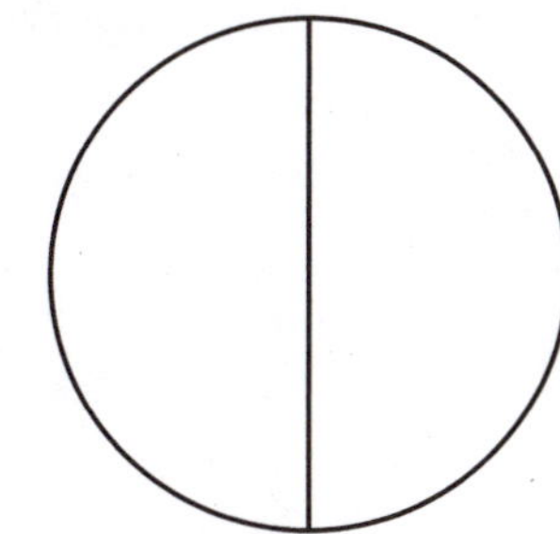

a. 2 and 3 b. 3 and 3 c. 2 and 2 d. 2 and 4

19. What is the number of triangles in the following figure?

a. 7 b. 8 c. 9 d. 10

20. What is the total number of slanting lines in the following figure?

a. 16 b. 18 c. 20 d. 22

Grouping

Grouping is the process of placing objects in one or more groups. Several types of questions may be asked based on grouping.

Choose the correct option in each of the following questions:

1. Identify the number of 2's group from the following pictures:

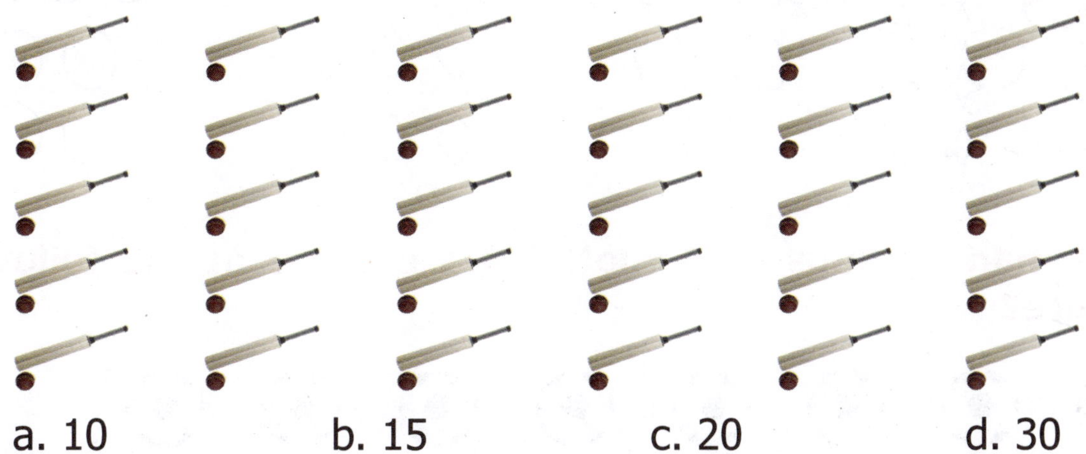

a. 10 b. 15 c. 20 d. 30

2. Number 5 belongs to ________.

P	Q	R
5, 15, 30, 100, 21 33, 10, 13, 19, 28 20, 24, 18, 68, 32	4, 7, 12, 18, 24 28, 7, 9, 38, 42 9, 36, 64, 63, 59	17, 52, 54, 8, 7 51, 41, 31, 21, 11 101, 116, 109, 89, 72

a. R group b. P and Q groups
c. P group d. P, Q and R groups

3. **How many groups of 2 pentagons and 2 stars can be formed from the shapes given below?**

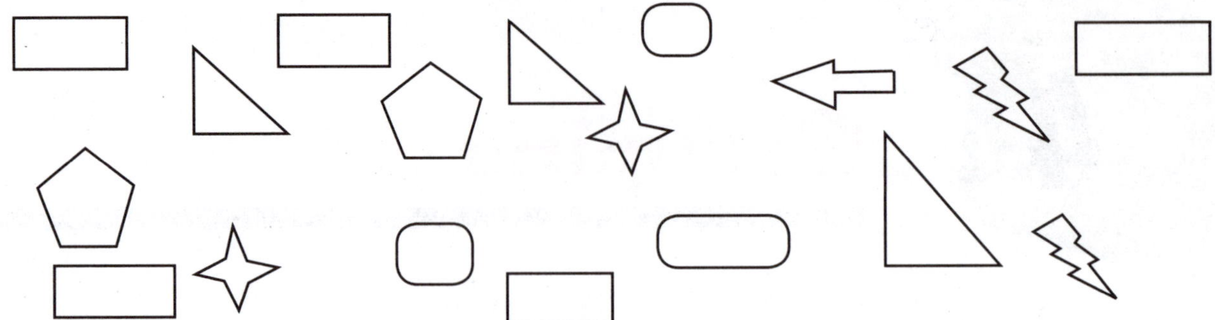

a. 5 group each b. 3 group each c. 2 group each d. 1 group each

4. **Identify the group of 4's:**

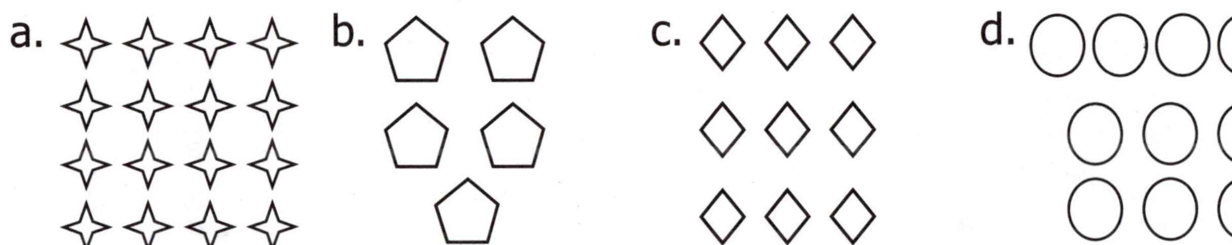

5. **How many groups of 4 footballs are there in the following picture?**

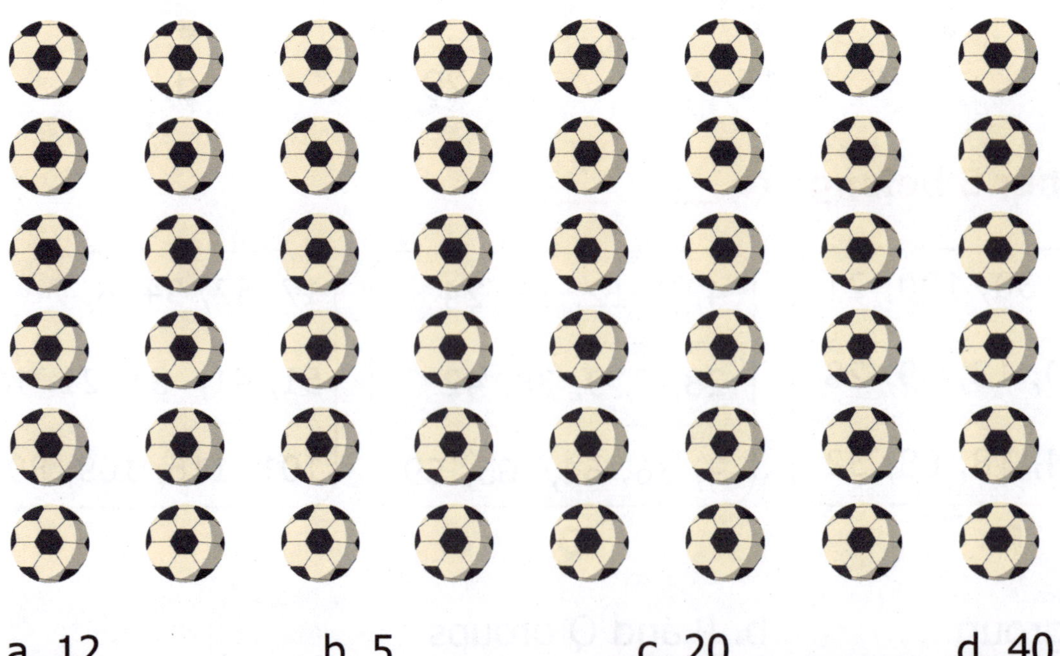

a. 12 b. 5 c. 20 d. 40

Direction: Look at the picture and answer the questions that follow:

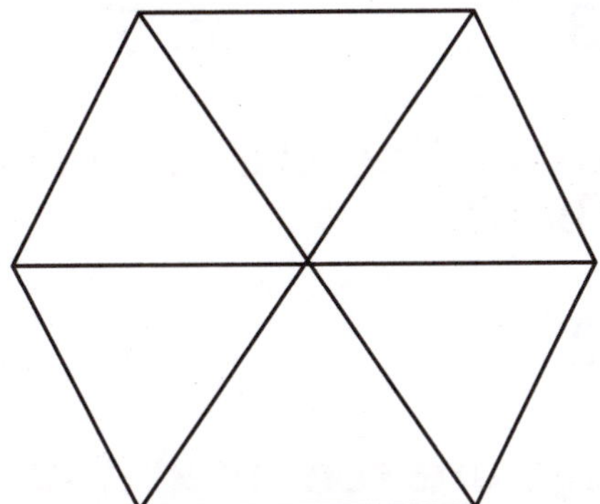

6. **How many more triangles are required if we want to make 4 groups of 3 triangles?**

a. 4   b. 6   c. 8   d. 3

7. **How many more triangles are required to complete 6 groups of 2 triangles?**

a. 4   b. 3   c. 5   d. 6

Direction: Look at the picture and answer the questions that follow:

8. **How many groups of 4 butterflies can be formed?**

a. 4   b. 5   c. 8   d. 6

9. **How many groups of 8 butterflies can be formed?**

a. 4 b. 3 c. 5 d. 7

10. **How many more butterflies are required if we want to make 3 groups of 9 butterflies?**

a. 1 b. 2 c. 3 d. 4

11. **How many more eggs are required if we want to form 3 groups of 7 eggs?**

a. 13 b. 4 c. 5 d. 6

12. **How many groups of 4 can be formed from the given caterpillars?**

a. 3 b. 5 c. 4 d. 6

13. **How many more caterpillars are required if we want to form 5 groups of 5 caterpillars?**

a. 3 b. 5 c. 4 d. 6

14. **Which is the correct description of the following picture?**

a. 5 groups of 3 fish

b. 2 groups of 5 fish

c. 3 groups of 5 fish

d. 2 group of 6 fish

15. **Which is the correct description of the following picture?**

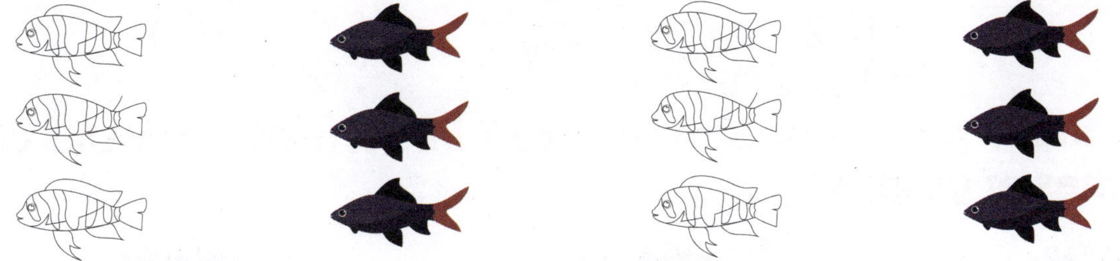

a. 2 groups of white and 2 groups of black fish

b. 3 groups of white and 4 groups of black fish

c. 5 groups of white and 4 groups of black fish

d. 3 groups of white and 3 groups of black fish

16. **Which is the correct description of the following picture?**

a. 3 groups of 3 apples and 2 groups of 3 pears

b. 2 groups of 3 apples, 2 groups of 3 pineapples, and 2 groups of 3 pears

c. 2 groups of 3 apples, 3 groups of 2 pineapples, 1 group of 3 bananas, and 2 groups of 3 pears

d. 3 groups of 3 apples, 3 groups of 3 pineapples, 1 group of 3 bananas, and 2 groups of 3 pears

17. How many more pears are required if we want to form 4 groups of 2 pears?

a. 1 b. 2 c. 3 d. 4

18. How many groups of 5 grapes can be formed from the given bunches of grapes?

a. 12 b. 6 c. 8 d. 20

19. How many groups of 3 stars are there?

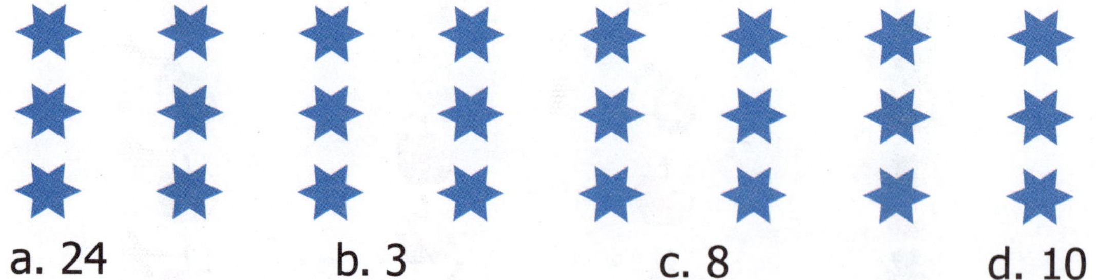

a. 24 b. 3 c. 8 d. 10

20. How many groups of 4 stars are there?

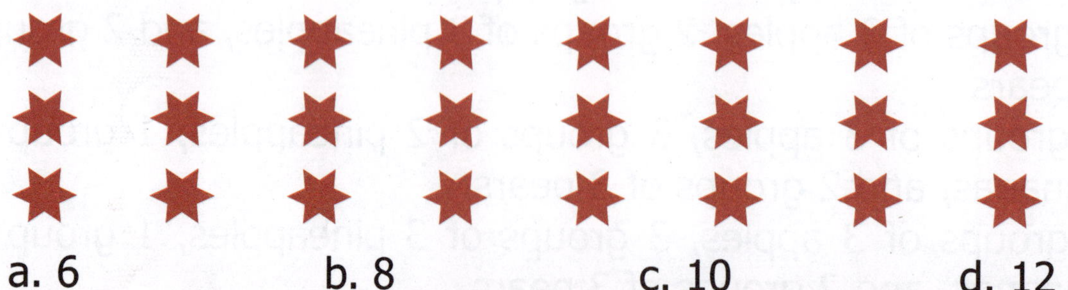

a. 6 b. 8 c. 10 d. 12

Special Understanding

Choose the correct option in each of the following questions:

1. ________ students are standing outside the bus.

a. 1 b. 2 c. 3 d. 4

2. Which bird is the nearest to the tree?

a. S b. P c. Q d. R

3. Which bird is the farthest from the tree?

a. S b. P c. Q d. R

4. **How many apples are there in basket B?**

a. 3 b. 4 c. 5 d. 6

5. **How many fruits, in total, are there in the baskets given below?**

a. 10 b. 12 c. 14 d. 15

6. **How many birds are flying above the clouds?**

a. 6 b. 4 c. 5 d. 3

7. **How many birds are flying on the left side of the tree?**

a. 3 b. 6 c. 5 d. 11

8. **How many birds are flying on the right side of the tree?**

a. 3 b. 6 c. 4 d. 9

9. **Number on the topmost step of the ladder is ________________.**

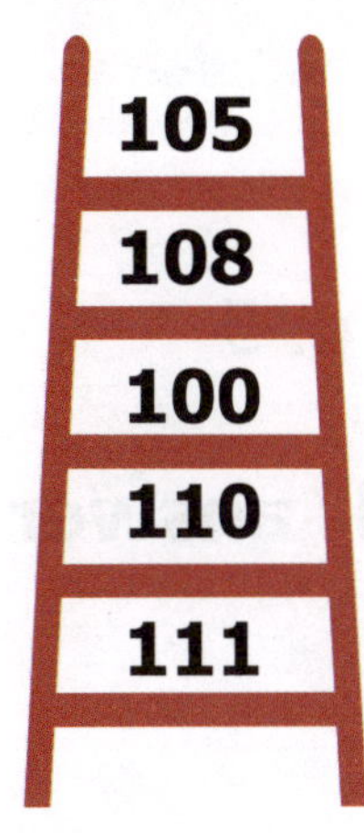

a. 111 b. 105 c. 100 d. 108

10. **Number on the second last step of the ladder is ________________.**

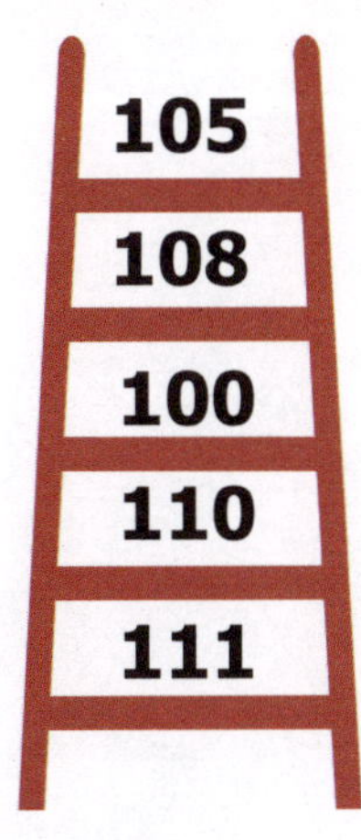

a. 111 b. 105 c. 110 d. 108

11. **Number of apples inside the bowl is ________________.**

a. 10 b. 9 c. 11 d. 12

12. Number of apples left after subtracting the apples outside the bowl from the apples inside the bowl is equal to ___________.

a. 6 b. 7 c. 10 d. 5

Direction: Observe the following picture and answer the questions 13 and 14:

13. How many flowers are there around the pond?

a. 2 b. 5 c. 6 d. 9

14. How many butterflies are there around the pond?

a. 2 b. 3 c. 6 d. 9

Direction: Observe the following picture carefully and answer the questions 15 and 16:

15. Which child is standing between T and V?

a. R b. V c. U d. W

16. Which child is standing between P and R?

a. W b. Q c. R d. P

17. How many apples are there on the tree?

a. 16 b. 4 c. 12 d. 14

18. What is the number of apples under the tree?

a. 16 b. 4 c. 12 d. 14

19. The tree is surrounded by ______________ gifts.

a. 4 b. 2 c. 5 d. 3

20. How many planes are flying above the cloud?

a. 7 b. 8 c. 9 d. 10

Ranking Test

Choose the correct option in each of the following questions:

1. The 5th ice cream from the right end is ice cream __________.

a. T b. S c. U d. R

2. The airplane that is 2nd from the left end is ______________.

a. P b. S c. J d. N

3. ____________ is fifth from the right end.

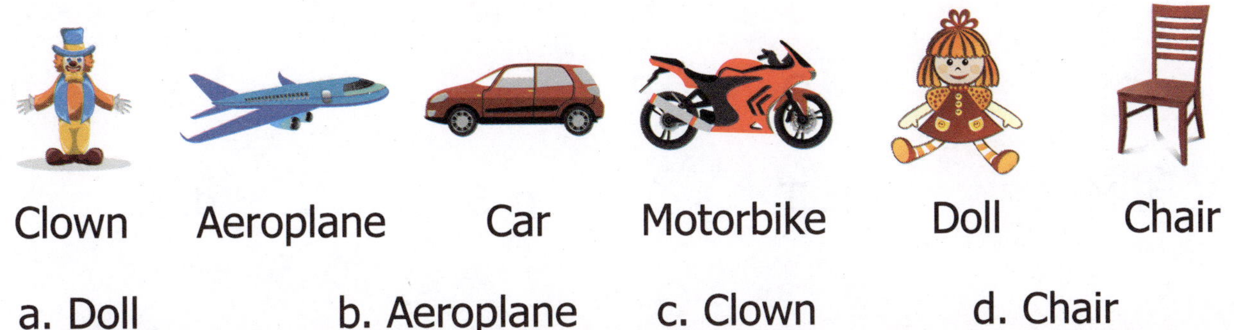

a. Doll b. Aeroplane c. Clown d. Chair

4. I am the third from the left end. I am a ________________.

Clown Aeroplane Car Motorbike Doll Chair

a. Car b. Motorbike c. Doll d. Aeroplane

5. The fourth puppy from the left end is ________________.

S U T Q V R P

a. V b. T c. P d. Q

6. I am the third from the left end and 10th from the right end. I am ________________.

Z Y X W V U T S R Q P O

a. X b. T c. Q d. W

7. I am the 8th from the left end and 1st from the right end. I am ________________.

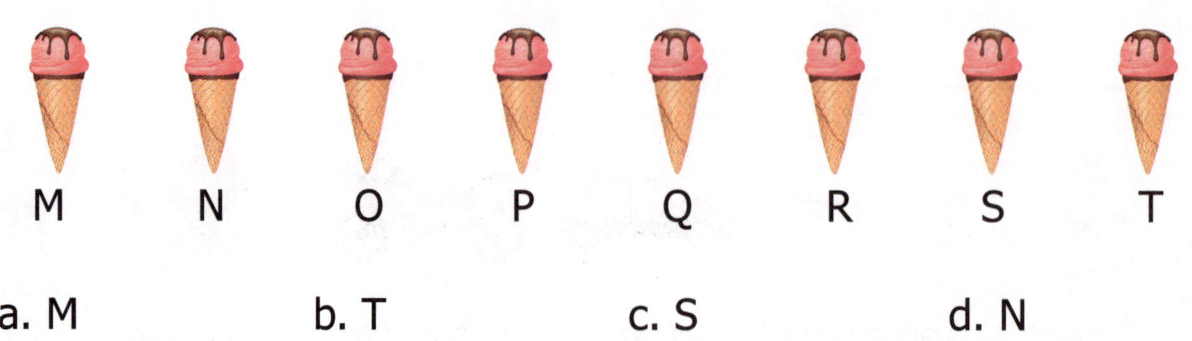

M N O P Q R S T

a. M b. T c. S d. N

8. **I am the 8th from the right end and 1st from the left end. I am ________________.**

a. M b. N c. P d. L

9. **The cub sitting at the third position from the right end is ________________.**

a. N b. P c. I d. J

10. **I am 4th from the left end and fifth from the right end. I am ________________.**

a. Ee b. Dd c. Cc d. Gg

11. **________________ is 7th from right end.**

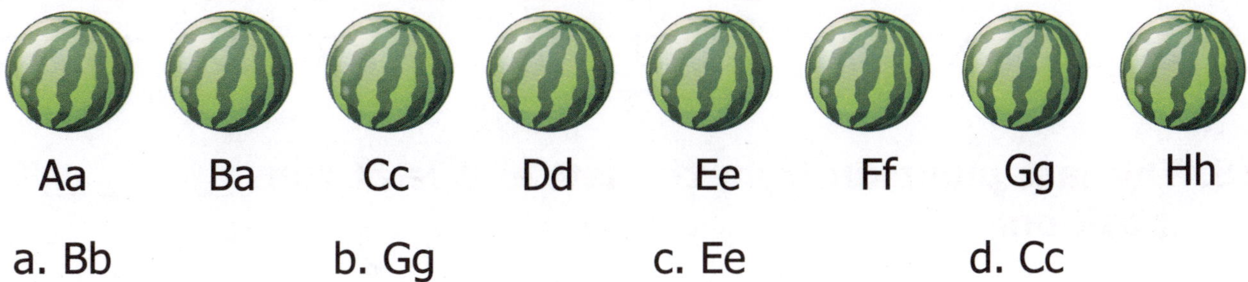

a. Bb b. Gg c. Ee d. Cc

Direction: Look at the picture given below and answer the questions that follow:

12. If umbrella K and M will interchange their positions, what will be the new position of umbrella K from the right end?

a. 6th b. 8th c. 9th d. 7th

13. If umbrella K and M will interchange their positions, what will be the new position of umbrella M from the left end?

a. 6th b. 5th c. 9th d. 7th

14. From the right end, the H umbrella is positioned at the ________________ position, and from the left end at the ________________ position.

a. 1st, 10th b. 10th, 1st c. 2nd, 10th d. 10th, 2nd

Direction: Look at the picture given below and answer the questions 15 and 16:

15. The last pumpkin from the left end is at the ________________ position.

a. 11th b. 13th c. 12th d. 10th

16. __________ is at the last position from the right end.

a. O b. Z c. Y d. P

17. What is the 4th figure from the right end?

a.  b.  c.  d.

18. The penguin that is in the first position from left end is ______________.

J S E M T ?

a. T b. M c. E d. J

19. The fifth letter from the left end is ________________.

P K O I G E B C D A

a. G b. P c. E d. J

20. The 8th letter from the right end is ______________.

P K O I G E B C D A

a. G b. P c. O d. K

Answer Key

Chapter 1

1. c	2. b	3. a	4. d
5. b	6. a	7. d	8. b
9. a	10. d	11. a	12. d
13. c	14. d	15. a	16. c
17. a	18. a	19. a	20. d

Chapter 2

1. a	2. b	3. c	4. d
5. a	6. b	7. c	8. d
9. a	10. b	11. c	12. d
13. a	14. b	15. c	16. a
17. c	18. d	19. b	20. b

Chapter 3

1. a	2. b	3. b	4. b
5. b	6. a	7. a	8. d
9. c	10. c	11. c	12. d
13. a	14. b	15. c	16. a
17. b	18. c	19. d	20. b

Chapter 4

1. b	2. c	3. d	4. a
5. a	6. b	7. d	8. d
9. b	10. c	11. d	12. b
13. b	14. b	15. a	16. c
17. b	18. b	19. c	20. a

Chapter 5

1. c	2. b	3. a	4. b
5. a	6. d	7. b	8. c
9. b	10. c	11. a	12. d
13. c	14. b	15. c	16. b
17. c	18. b	19. d	20. a

Chapter 6

1. b	2. c	3. b	4. a
5. d	6. a	7. b	8. c
9. d	10. b	11. a	12. d
13. b	14. a	15. c	16. b
17. d	18. d	19. a	20. c